Reading/Writing Companion

Mc
Graw
Hill

mheducation.com/prek-12

Copyright © 2023 McGraw Hill

Send all inquiries to:
McGraw Hill
1325 Avenue of the Americas
New York, NY 10019

ISBN: 978-1-26-574630-8
MHID: 1-26-574630-3

Printed in the United States of America.

5 6 7 8 9 LMN 26 25 24 23 22   A

Welcome to
WONDERS!

We're here to help you set goals to build on the amazing things you already know. We'll also help you reflect on everything you'll learn.

Let's start by taking a look at the incredible things you'll do this year.

You'll build knowledge on exciting topics and find answers to interesting questions.

You'll read fascinating fiction, informational texts, and poetry and respond to what you read with your own thoughts and ideas.

And you'll research and write stories, poems, and essays of your own!

Here's a sneak peek at how you'll do it all.

"Let's go!"

You'll explore new ideas by reading groups of different texts about the same topic. These groups of texts are called *text sets*.

At the beginning of a text set, we'll help you set goals on the My Goals page. You'll see a bar with four boxes beneath each goal. Think about what you already know to fill in the bar. Here's an example.

I can read and understand realistic fiction.

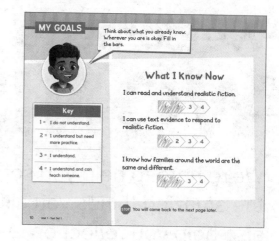

As you move through a text set, you'll explore an essential question and build your knowledge of a topic until you're ready to write about it yourself.

You'll also learn skills that will help you reach your text set goals. At the end of lessons, you'll see a new Check In bar with four boxes.

CHECK IN 1 2 3 4

Reflect on how well you understood a lesson to fill in the bar.

Here are some questions you can ask yourself.

- Was I able to complete the task?

- Was it easy or was it hard?

- Do I think I need more practice?

You have plenty of tools and resources to learn more, such as anchor charts and center activities. You can also reread a lesson or ask a teacher or peer for help.

It's okay if I think I need more practice. The most important thing is that I do my best and keep learning!

Thinking about what works best for me helps me choose what to do next.

At the end of each text set, you'll show off the knowledge you built by completing a fun task. Then you'll return to the second My Goals page where we'll help you reflect on all that you learned.

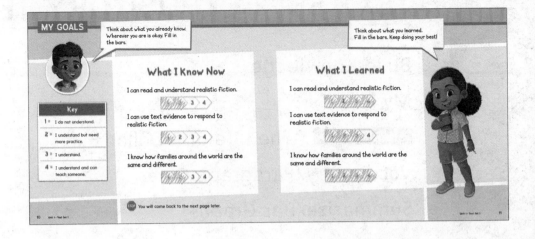

"Let's get started!"

TEXT SET 1 **EXPOSITORY TEXT**

TEXT SET 2 DRAMA/MYTH

TEXT SET 3 **POETRY**

Samuel Borges Photography/Shutterstock

EXTENDED WRITING

CONNECT AND REFLECT

 Digital Tools

Find this eBook and other resources at **my.mheducation.com**

Vitaly Korovin/Shutterstock

Build Knowledge

? Essential Question
How do we use money?

Build Vocabulary

 Write new words you learned about how we use our money. Draw lines and circles for the words you write.

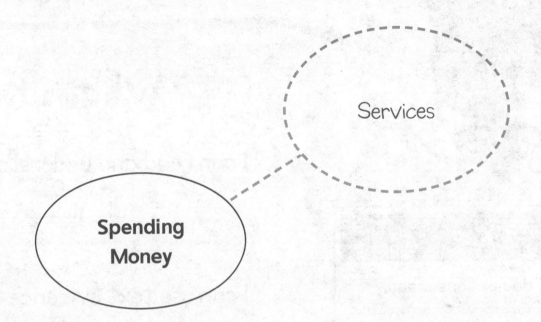

Services

Spending Money

 Go online to **my.mheducation.com** and read the "Making Dollars and Cents" Blast. Think about how money is made. Then blast back your response.

Think about what you already know. Fill in the bars. You'll learn more with practice.

What I Know Now

I can read and understand expository text.

1 > 2 > 3 > 4

I can use text evidence to respond to expository text.

I know about how we use money.

1 > 2 > 3 > 4

Key

1 =.	I do not understand.
2 =	I understand but need more practice.
3 =	I understand.
4 =	I understand and can teach someone.

STOP You will come back to the next page later.

Think about what you learned. Fill in the bars. What is getting easier for you?

What I Learned

I can read and understand expository text.

1 2 3 4

I can use text evidence to respond to expository text.

1 2 3 4

I know about how we use money.

1 2 3 4

My Goal
I can read and understand expository text.

TAKE NOTES

As you read, write down interesting words and important information.

_____
_____
_____
_____
_____
_____
_____
_____

The Life of a Dollar Bill

Essential Question

?

How do we use money?

Read to learn about how a dollar bill circulates.

(t) McGraw-Hill Education; (c)Jacobs Stock Photography/Photodisc/Getty Images

The Dollar Bill Is Printed

One day, a dollar bill is printed at the United States Bureau of Engraving and Printing. The bill is printed on a machine that was **invented**, or created, to save time. It prints many bills at a time.

The U.S. Bureau of Engraving and Printing prints bills each day.

Let's follow the dollar bill. It gets sent to a big bank and then a local bank. A family visits this neighborhood bank to get **money**. The dollar bill goes to a boy for his allowance.

The boy brings the dollar bill to the bookstore. He checks **prices** to see how much the books cost. Then he decides what he can **purchase**. He finds a book to buy, but is it **worth** the price? He's not sure. The boy reads the back of the book and thinks about the price. The boy decides the book is a good **value**, so he exchanges his money for the book.

(t) Joe Raedle/Getty Images News/Getty Images; (b) McGraw-Hill Education

FIND TEXT EVIDENCE 🔍

Read

Paragraph 2

Paragraph Clues

Write a clue to the meaning of *local* from the paragraph.

neighborhood bill

was made in Engraving

Paragraph 3

Central Idea and Details

Draw a box around how the boy decides the book is a good value.

Reread

Author's Craft

How do the photograph and caption help you understand how dollar bills are printed?

Read

Paragraphs 1–2

Summarize

Underline details that tell how the girl receives and uses the bill. Summarize how the bill travels.

the dollar bill

stars with boy and

it end up with

the girl and

it end with

man

Graph

Bar Graphs

Circle the bar in the graph that shows the average life span of a dollar bill.

Reread

Author's Craft

How does the author help you understand when a dollar bill is no longer usable?

The Dollar Bill Travels

Later, a girl buys a birthday card at the bookstore. She gets the dollar bill as change. She takes the dollar bill home and saves it in her piggy bank.

When the girl wants to see a movie, she takes money out of her piggy bank, including the dollar bill. She uses it to pay for the ticket. Then the dollar bill travels on.

Over five years pass and now a man gets the dollar bill. It is worn out and torn. The man is not sure if it's usable. What happens to the ripped bill? The man takes it to his local bank and trades it in for a new dollar bill.

The Average Life Span of U.S. Bills

Number of Years

10 9 8 7 6 5 4 3 2 1 0

| $1 bill | $5 bill | $10 bill | $20 bill | $50 bill |

As of December 2013 • Source: U.S. Federal Reserve

The Dollar Bill Is Replaced

The old dollar bill is returned to the big bank where workers decide that it can't be used again. They destroy the bill by shredding it. They cut it into tiny pieces.

A machine shreds over 6 billion worn-out bills a year.

Back at the U.S. Bureau of Engraving and Printing, a new dollar bill is printed to replace the old one. Workers use a **record** to keep track of how many bills are printed and destroyed. They make sure there are enough bills in the **system** so people can buy and sell things.

The next time you hold a one-dollar bill, think of where it has been and where it is going. Each dollar bill has a busy, useful life.

Retell

Use your notes and think about the events in "The Life of a Dollar Bill." Then retell the most important events.

EXPOSITORY TEXT

FIND TEXT EVIDENCE

Read

Paragraph 1

Summarize

Circle details that tell what happens to the old dollar bill. Summarize the events.

the dollar it at the Bank it go to the Boy it go to the girl it go to the man it get shr-eding

Paragraph 2

Central Idea and Details

Underline text evidence that explains why the U.S. Bureau of Engraving and Printing replaces the old bill.

Reread

Author's Craft

In the last paragraph, how does the author leave you thinking more about a dollar bill's busy, useful life?

Vocabulary

Use the sentences to talk with a partner about each word. Then answer the questions.

invented

Thomas Edison **invented** the light bulb.

What are other useful things people invented?

_____

_____

money

A dollar bill is **money** made of paper.

What coins do we use as money?

_____

_____

> **Build Your Word List** Choose an interesting word that you noted while reading. Look up and write its definition using a print or online dictionary.

prices

Marsha looked at the **prices** of sneakers.

Do you know the prices of any food items or toys?

_____

_____

purchase

Sam will **purchase** a snack.

What is something you would like to purchase?

_____

_____

record

Our teacher keeps a **record** of who comes to school every day.

What is something you keep a record of?

_____

_____

system

Our teacher has a **system** for organizing our writing materials.

What is something you have a system for?

_____

_____

value

A quarter has a greater **value** than a dime.

What is a coin that has a greater value than a penny?

_____

_____

worth

The jewels are **worth** a lot of money.

What is something that is worth a small amount of money?

_____

_____

Paragraph Clues

Look for paragraph clues when you read a new word. These words and sentences in the paragraph can help you figure out the meaning of the word.

FIND TEXT EVIDENCE

I'll use paragraph clues to figure out what shredding *means. In the first sentence, I see the old bill can't be used again. The last sentence says* shredding *means "to cut it into tiny pieces."*

> The old dollar bill is returned to the big bank where workers decide that it can't be used again. They destroy the bill by shredding it. They cut it into tiny pieces.

Your Turn Use paragraph clues to figure out the meaning of the words below.

change, page 14 _____

_____

torn, page 14 _____

CHECK IN ▶ 1 ⟩ 2 ⟩ 3 ⟩ 4 ⟩

Martin Poole/Photographer's Choice/Getty Images

Summarize

To summarize a selection, you tell only the most important details of the selection. This helps you remember what you have read.

🔍 **FIND TEXT EVIDENCE**

After I read page 13 of "The Life of a Dollar Bill," I will summarize what I read to make sure I understand it.

Quick Tip

Locate the details that will help you to understand what the author explains or describes. Then connect these details in your own words to summarize the text.

Page 13

> Let's follow the dollar bill. It gets sent to a big bank and then a local bank. A family visits this neighborhood bank to get money. The dollar bill goes to a boy for his allowance.

I read that a dollar bill is printed and sent to a big bank and then to a local bank. The dollar bill then goes to a boy.

Your Turn Reread the last paragraph on page 13. Then summarize the information.

_____

_____

_____

CHECK IN 1 2 3 4

Bar Graphs

"The Life of a Dollar Bill" is an expository text. It gives facts and information about a topic. The author uses text features such as a bar graph.

FIND TEXT EVIDENCE

I know that "The Life of a Dollar Bill" is an expository text. It gives information about money. The text features help me learn more about dollar bills.

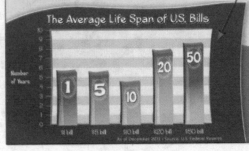

Page 14

The Dollar Bill Travels

Later, a girl buys a birthday card at the bookstore. She gets the dollar bill as change. She takes the dollar bill home and saves it in her piggy bank.

When the girl wants to see a movie, she takes money out of her piggy bank, including the dollar bill. She uses it to pay for the ticket. Then the dollar bill travels on.

Over five years pass and now a man gets the dollar bill. It is worn out and torn. The man is not sure if it's usable. What happens to the ripped bill? The man takes it to his local bank and trades it in for a new dollar bill.

The Average Life Span of U.S. Bills

Graph

A bar graph helps you compare information using numbers.

Your Turn What two bills in the graph have the longest life spans? How do you know?

COLLABORATE

_____

_____

CHECK IN 1 > 2 > 3 > 4

Central Idea and Relevant Details

The central idea is the most important point, or idea, about the topic. Relevant details support the central idea.

🔍 FIND TEXT EVIDENCE

As I reread page 14, I understand that a relevant detail is that a bill gets old, worn out, and torn.

Detail

A dollar bill is worn out
and torn.

 Your Turn Continue rereading the selection. Fill in the graphic organizer with relevant details and the central idea.

CHECK IN 1 2 3 4

Detail

A dollar bill is worn out and torn.

Detail

a dollar bill is give to a boy for his allowance.

Detail

Later a girl gets a birth day card at the bookstore she gets the dollar bill

Central Idea

iss about want a dollar bill cahi duw

Respond to Reading

COLLABORATE

Talk about the prompt below. Use your notes and text evidence to support your response.

How does the selection help you understand the life of a dollar bill?

_____

_____

_____

_____

_____

_____

_____

_____

Quick Tip

Use these sentence starters to help you organize your text evidence.

The events in the life of a dollar bill...

First, I learned that...

Then, a dollar bill...

Finally, a dollar is...

Grammar Connections

Add an apostrophe (') and *-s* to a singular noun to show who or what has something.

The girl has a piggy bank. A dollar bill is in the girl's piggy bank.

CHECK IN ⟩ 1 ⟩ 2 ⟩ 3 ⟩ 4 ⟩

Producers and Consumers

COLLABORATE

With a partner, create a money flowchart that shows how people are both producers and consumers. Follow the research process to create your flowchart.

Step 1 **Set a Goal** Decide on ways people earn and spend money that you will show. Write two ideas below:

_____

_____

_____

Step 2 **Identify Sources** Relevant sources about how people earn and spend money are books, magazine articles, or websites.

Step 3 **Find and Record Information** Take notes in your own words. Always cite your sources.

Step 4 **Organize and Combine Information** Organize information in sequential order. You may set up events in a circle to show how money circulates, or passes from person to person in a cycle.

Step 5 **Create and Present** Draw or use photos to show each event in the flowchart. Take turns presenting parts of your flowchart with the class.

Quick Tip

Remember that people are called *producers* when they earn money and *consumers* when they spend money.

Tetra images/Punchstock

CHECK IN 1 2 3 4

Money Madness

? **How does the author share information in a way that gets your attention?**

Literature Anthology: pages 490–509

COLLABORATE

Talk About It Reread pages 492–493. Discuss ways that the author uses language to keep you interested in the text.

Cite Text Evidence Use the text details on pages 492–493 to complete the chart below.

Make Inferences

Why does the author want you to imagine a world without money?

Page Number	Example	How the Author Keeps Your Attention
492	"Now, imagine a world without money."	The author gives the reader a direct command.
492	"...how would you buy a loaf of bread?"	
493	"...you would have to make them."	

Write The author keeps my attention by _____

_____

CHECK IN 1 2 3 4

? **How does the author help you understand why coins and paper money were invented?**

COLLABORATE

Talk About It Reread pages 499–500. Talk with a partner about what you learned about money.

Cite Text Evidence Write about how the author uses illustrations and details to explain why coins and paper money were invented.

Page 499	Page 500

Write The author helps me understand that _____

_____

_____

Quick Tip

As you read, use these sentence starters to talk about money.

Rocks come in different sizes but...

Coins can be...

Carrying many coins is...

Paper money is...

 Combine Information

What are some of the earliest forms of money? Why were metal coins easier to use than these forms of money?

CHECK IN 1 2 3 4

? **How does the graphic on page 505 help you understand the information in the text?**

COLLABORATE
Talk About It Reread page 505. Describe the steps involved in buying things online.

Cite Text Evidence Use the Venn diagram to tell the similarities and differences between paper money and digital money.

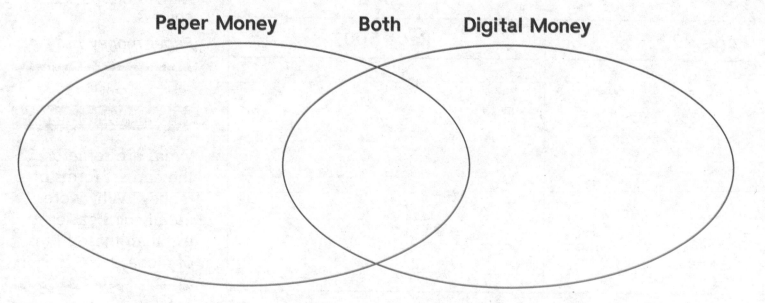

Paper Money   Both   Digital Money

Write The graphic on page 505 helps me understand

_____

_____

_____

CHECK IN 〉 1 〉 2 〉 3 〉 4 〉

Respond to Reading

COLLABORATE Discuss the prompt below. Use your notes and text evidence to support your opinion.

Do you think bartering or using paper money is a better way for people to get things they need?

_____

_____

_____

_____

_____

_____

_____

Quick Tip

Use these sentence starters to organize your text evidence.

Long ago, people...

Then people traded...

Early forms of money were...

People used...

People needed better forms of money because...

CHECK IN 1 2 3 4

King Midas and the Golden Touch

Literature Anthology: pages 510–511

Many years ago, King Midas lived in a grand palace with a beautiful rose garden. He had one daughter whom he loved very much.

One day, King Midas performed a good deed for a friend, who rewarded King Midas by granting him one wish. King Midas wanted to become rich, but he did not desire money. He did not want to purchase jewels and goods. Instead, he wanted riches that money could not buy. King Midas wished that everything he touched be turned instantly to gold.

Reread the first two paragraphs of the story. **Draw a box** around the description of where the king lives.

What main event takes place in the beginning of the story?

Underline two details that show what King Midas wants. **Circle** the wish King Midas makes.

Discuss why the author begins the story by describing where King Midas lives. Use text evidence to support your ideas.

King Midas reached for the food and water on his gold table. But each object he touched turned to gold, leaving him hungry and thirsty.

King Midas's daughter offered him her water. He reached to take it and, without thinking, touched her hand. Immediately, she turned to gold, too! King Midas begged his friend, "Undo my wish, please!" Seeing that he had learned his lesson, his friend undid the wish at once. All the golden objects returned to normal, including his daughter.

King Midas hugged his daughter tightly. He had lost his gold, but he had gained back what he truly loved. Some things are worth more than gold.

Reread the rest of the story. In paragraphs 1 and 2, **circle** text evidence that shows how King Midas's wish becomes a problem.

Underline why the friend undoes the wish. How does this resolve, or solve, King Midas's problem?

_____

_____

_____

Draw a box around the lesson King Midas learns at the end of the story.

COLLABORATE

Discuss how the setting of the dinner table is used to show how King Midas's wish becomes a problem.

Reread | PAIRED SELECTION

? **Why does the author begin and end the story telling about the king's love for his daughter?**

Talk About It With a partner, describe King Midas at the beginning of the myth. Then describe him at the end.

Cite Text Evidence Who does King Midas love? What does he want? Write text evidence from the story.

Page	Text Evidence

Write The author begins and ends the story by telling about the king's love for his daughter because _____

_____

_____

> **Quick Tip**
>
> Text evidence about King Midas's love for his daughter will help you figure out the story's theme.

CHECK IN 1 > 2 > 3 > 4 >

Character and Events

Action verbs and describing words help readers understand the actions of the characters and story events.

🔍 **FIND TEXT EVIDENCE**

In paragraph 2 of page 29, the author uses the verb *begged*. It shows how strongly King Midas wants his wish to be undone. It also helps show that he has learned his lesson.

> King Midas begged his friend, "Undo my wish, please!" Seeing that he had learned his lesson, his friend undid the wish at once.

Your Turn Reread the first sentence of the last paragraph on page 29. What words describe what the king does?

_____

How does this description help you to understand the way King Midas feels?

_____

_____

CHECK IN ▸ 1 ⟩ 2 ⟩ 3 ⟩ 4 ⟩

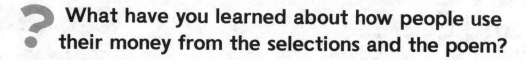

? **What have you learned about how people use their money from the selections and the poem?**

Talk About It Read the poem, "The Lemonade Stand." Talk with a partner about what happens in the poem. What does Sally do during the summer?

Cite Text Evidence With a partner, **underline** what Sally does all summer long. **Circle** what Sally does with the money she has earned.

Write The selections I read and this poem help me understand _____

_____

_____

_____

_____

_____

Quick Tip

Use these sentence starters to talk about what people do with their money.
People need money...
People can spend...
People can save...
People think about...

The Lemonade Stand

Sally opened up a stand
Where she sold lemonade.
She worked all summer long
And for her hard work, was paid.

Sally took the money she earned
Wearing a smile from ear to ear.
She brought it to the bank
To save for the next school year!

CHECK IN 〉 1 〉 2 〉 3 〉 4 〉

Give Tips about Money

Think about the ideas about money in the texts you read. Think about the decisions people make about spending and saving money. What should kids learn about money?

1. Look at your Build Knowledge notes in your reader's notebook.

2. Write a list of tips kids should think about when it comes to money. Describe how to make smart decisions about saving and spending. You may even remind kids about the things they should value more than money.

3. Include some of the new words you learned. Be sure to use examples from three of the texts you read in your list of tips.

Think about what you learned in this text set. Fill in the bars on page 11.

Build Knowledge

Essential Question

What do myths help us understand?

Build Vocabulary

Write new words you learned about what myths help us understand. Draw lines and circles for the words you write.

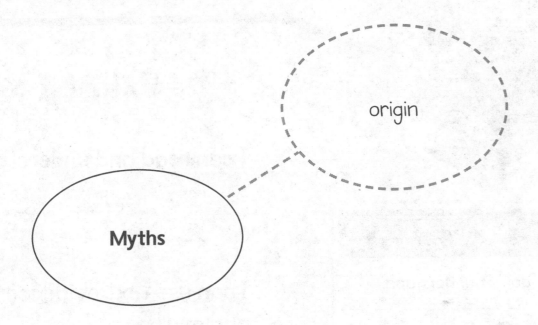

origin

Myths

Go online to **my.mheducation.com** and read the "Plants that Grow into Myths" Blast. Think about how myths can explain the importance of plants in a culture. Then blast back your response.

Think about what you already know.
Fill in the bars. Keep doing your best!

What I Know Now

Key
1 = I do not understand.
2 = I understand but need more practice.
3 = I understand.
4 = I understand and can teach someone.

I can read and understand a drama and myth.

1 > 2 > 3 > 4

I can use text evidence to respond to a drama and myth.

1 > 2 > 3 > 4

I know about what myths can help us understand.

1 > 2 > 3 > 4

STOP You will come back to the next page later.

> Think about what you learned. Fill in the bars. You can always improve so keep trying!

What I Learned

I can read and understand a drama and myth.

1 > 2 > 3 > 4

I can use text evidence to respond to a drama and myth.

1 > 2 > 3 > 4

I know about what myths can help us understand.

1 > 2 > 3 > 4

My Goal I can read and understand a drama and myth.

TAKE NOTES

As you read, make note of interesting words and important events.

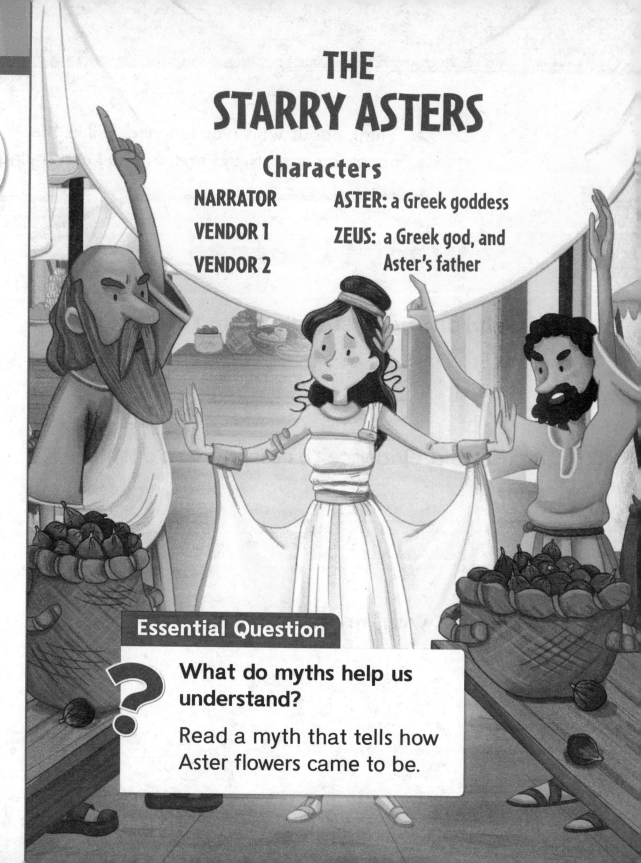

THE STARRY ASTERS

Characters

NARRATOR

VENDOR 1

VENDOR 2

ASTER: a Greek goddess

ZEUS: a Greek god, and Aster's father

Essential Question

? What do myths help us understand?

Read a myth that tells how Aster flowers came to be.

SCENE ONE

Long ago, in a marketplace in Athens, Greece.

NARRATOR: There came a time when gods and goddesses no longer wanted to live with people. There was too much fighting. Farmers fought over their **crops**. Vendors fought over who had the right to sell figs.

VENDOR 1: My figs are the most delicious in Athens!

VENDOR 2: No! *My* figs are better! You will *never* sell figs in this city!

NARRATOR: Aster, the last goddess on Earth, asked them to stop fighting. She tried to help them **develop** ways to get along. They refused to see the light.

ASTER: Please! Let me speak my mind. There is room for you both here in Athens! (*Pointing to Vendor 1*) You may sell figs at the **edge** of the city. (*Pointing to Vendor 2*) You may sell figs in the city center!

VENDOR 1: (*Shaking his head*) I smell a rat! The vendor who sells in the city center will have many more customers!

VENDOR 2: No! The vendor who sells at the city's edge will reach all the customers who travel into Athens!

NARRATOR: This was the last straw for Aster. She knew they could not agree. It was time to leave.

FIND TEXT EVIDENCE 🔍

Read

Elements of a Drama

Circle the characters' names. Write the setting for Scene 1.

_____

_____

Scene 1

Reread

Underline what Aster asks each vendor to do. Reread and explain their responses.

_____

_____

Reread

Author's Craft

How does the author use dialogue to show the way Aster feels?

FIND TEXT EVIDENCE

Read

Scene 2

Make Inferences

Why does Zeus ask Aster if she's sure about her decision?

_____

_____

_____

Scene 2

Theme

Underline what Aster wants to do. **Circle** the detail in the Narrator's line that supports why Aster wants to do this.

Reread

Author's Craft

How does the author use stage directions to help you visualize the characters?

SCENE TWO

A hill overlooking Athens at night.

ASTER: (*Looking up*) Father, I wish to live among the **shining** stars!

ZEUS: (*Speaking from the sky*) Aster, the people on Earth have gone through many **stages**. There was a time when they got along. Now is a time when they fight. One day they will get along again. Are you sure you wish to leave them?

NARRATOR: Aster looked around at Earth's beauty. A gentle breeze **rustled** the green leaves on tree branches. The stars shone **golden** on the sea. But down in the city, the people argued and fought.

ASTER: (*Sadly*) Yes, Father. I want to live in the starry sky.

SCENE THREE

In the night sky above ancient Greece.

NARRATOR: The next night, Zeus woke Aster from her long slumber.

ZEUS: Daughter, it is night! It is time to sparkle like a star for the people of Earth.

ASTER: (*Looking down*) Oh no, Father! When I lived on Earth, I could look up at the night sky and see the stars. But I see no stars when I look down upon Earth!

ZEUS: I am sorry, Aster. But you are part of the sky now. You have a purpose here.

NARRATOR: Aster began to cry. Her sparkling tears fell to the land below and soaked into the soil.

ASTER: (*Crying*) Have I had a change of heart? Have I made a mistake? Will I never see the beautiful stars again?

ZEUS: Only you can answer that, dear daughter.

NARRATOR: Aster looked down at Earth. In the places where her tears landed, star-shaped flowers **appeared**. The meadows were soon covered in the flowers we now call *asters*.

Retell

Use your notes and think about the events in "The Starry Asters." Retell the plot of the myth.

FIND TEXT EVIDENCE

Read

Scene 3

Idioms

Circle the phrase in Aster's first question that means "to change the way you think or feel about something." Why does Aster ask this question?

_____

_____

Reread

Author's Craft

How does the author conclude the final scene?

Vocabulary

Talk with a partner about each word. Then answer the questions.

appeared

Buds **appeared** on the tree in early spring.

What else do you think appeared in spring?

_____

_____

crops

The farmer grows **crops** of corn and wheat.

What are some other crops?

_____

_____

_____

Build Your Word List Circle *sparkling* on page 41. Write synonyms and antonyms for *sparkling* in your reader's notebook. You may use an online thesaurus to help you.

develop

The tadpole will **develop** into a frog.

What is another word for develop?

_____

_____

edge

The ball rolled off the **edge** of the table.

Is the edge close to or far from the center of the table?

_____

_____

golden

The **golden** Sun shone in the blue sky.

Name some things that are golden.

_____

_____

_____

rustled

The leaves **rustled** in the wind.

What else can be rustled?

_____

_____

shining

The **shining** flashlight made it easier to see in the dark.

What other things are shining?

_____

_____

stages

Egg, caterpillar, and butterfly are **stages** in a butterfly's life.

What is one of the stages in a cat's life?

_____

_____

Idioms

Idioms are words or phrases that have different meanings than the real meanings of the words.

FIND TEXT EVIDENCE

I read on page 39 that the vendors "refused to see the light." The phrase see the light is an idiom because they aren't closing their eyes. They refuse to understand how they can get along. I think "to see the light" here means "to understand something."

They refused to see the light.

Your Turn Use context clues to figure out the meaning of this idiom.

the last straw, page 39 _____

_____

_____

CHECK IN 1 2 3 4

Reread

As you read, stop and check that you can ask and answer questions about the story. If not, reread these parts to make sure you understand.

Quick Tip

You may need to reread a paragraph more than once to understand the language or ideas.

🔍 **FIND TEXT EVIDENCE**

I didn't understand why the people were fighting. I will reread page 39 to find out why.

Page 39

There came a time when gods and goddesses no longer wanted to live with people. There was too much fighting. Farmers fought over their **crops**. Vendors fought over who had the right to sell figs.

I read the narrator explain how the farmers fight about crops. The vendors fight about who is allowed to sell figs. This explains why the people are fighting.

Your Turn Why does Vendor 2 refuse to sell figs in the city center? Reread page 39 to find the answer.

_____

_____

_____

CHECK IN 1 ⟩ 2 ⟩ 3 ⟩ 4 ⟩

Elements of a Drama

"The Starry Asters" is a drama, or a play, that tells a myth. It has parts that the characters speak aloud. Stage directions can tell about the setting or the characters' actions.

The author uses a narrator to tell important details about the characters, setting, and events.

🔍 FIND TEXT EVIDENCE

I see that "The Starry Asters" is a drama. It is organized in parts called scenes, and there are stage directions. The characters' names are in capital letters before dialogue.

Page 39

SCENE ONE

Long ago, in a marketplace in Athens, Greece.

NARRATOR: There came a time when gods and goddesses no longer wanted to live with people. There was too much fighting. Farmers fought over their **crops**. Vendors fought over who had the right to sell figs.

VENDOR 1: My figs are the most delicious in Athens!

VENDOR 2: No! *My* figs are better! You will *never* sell figs in this city!

NARRATOR: Aster, the last goddess on Earth, asked them to stop fighting. She tried to help them **develop** ways to get along. They refused to see the light.

ASTER: Please! Let me speak my mind. There is room for you both here in Athens! (*Pointing to Vendor 1*) You may sell figs at the **edge** of the city. (*Pointing to Vendor 2*) You may sell figs in the city center!

VENDOR 1: (*Shaking his head*) I smell a rat! The vendor who sells in the city center will have many more customers!

VENDOR 2: No! The vendor who sells at the city's edge will reach all the customers who travel in to Athens!

NARRATOR: This was the last straw for Aster. She knew they could not agree. It was time to leave.

Dialogue

I see that each character has dialogue, or the words the character says in the play.

COLLABORATE

Your Turn Reread Scene 3. Where does the author name the setting? What is the importance of this setting to the story?

_____

_____

_____

_____

CHECK IN 1 2 3 4

Theme

The theme of a story is the big idea, or message, the author wants to tell the reader. To find the theme, think about what the characters say and do.

🔍 FIND TEXT EVIDENCE

As I reread page 39, I read that the fighting continued to upset Aster. She knew it was time to leave. This clue gives me an idea about the theme.

> **Clue**
>
> The vendors keep fighting, so Aster wants to leave Earth.

Your Turn Continue reading "The Starry Asters." Fill in additional clues and the theme in the graphic organizer.

Quick Tip

Ask questions about the characters to figure out clues and the theme. For example: *Why does the character say this? How does Aster feel now? What has she learned?*

CHECK IN 1 2 3 4

Clue

The vendors keep fighting,
so Aster wants to leave Earth.

↓

Clue

↓

Clue

↓

Theme

Respond to Reading

Talk about the prompt below. Use your notes and text evidence to support your response.

How does the theme of the play develop from the dialogue of the characters?

_____

_____

_____

_____

_____

_____

_____

Quick Tip

Use these sentence starters to help you organize your text evidence.

Aster and the vendors...

Zeus and Aster...

The narrator says...

Grammar Connections

Remember to use an **apostrophe (')** with a contraction to show where a letter or letters are missing.

For example:

I'm = I am

you're = you are

It's = It is

they're = they are

CHECK IN 1 2 3 4

Plants

With a partner, create a diagram that answers the research question: *How do the parts of a plant work together to meet the plant's needs?* Follow the research process to create your diagram.

Quick Tip

As you take notes for your plant diagram, use pictures, words, and numbers to record and organize your information.

Step 1 **Set a Goal** Decide on a plant for your diagram.

Write your topic: _____

Step 2 **Identify Sources** Find out how each part of the plant keeps it healthy. Relevant sources can be books, magazine articles, or websites.

Step 3 **Find and Record Information** Take notes on information you find. Be sure to write down the sources of the information.

Step 4 **Organize and Combine Information** Organize details about each of the plant's parts and their functions, or what they do. Explain how different parts might work together.

Step 5 **Create and Present** Draw your final diagram. Label each plant part and write information about how it helps to keep the plant healthy. Take turns as you present the plant diagram to the class.

CHECK IN 1 2 3 4

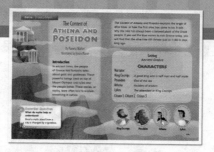

The Contest of Athena and Poseidon

Literature Anthology: pages 512–527

 How does the author use stage directions and dialogue to develop the characters?

 Talk About It Reread pages 516–517. Discuss what you learn about Athena and Poseidon.

Cite Text Evidence Compare and contrast the characters. Fill in the diagram with text evidence.

Make Inferences

Why is Athena amused when she speaks to Poseidon? Make an inference.

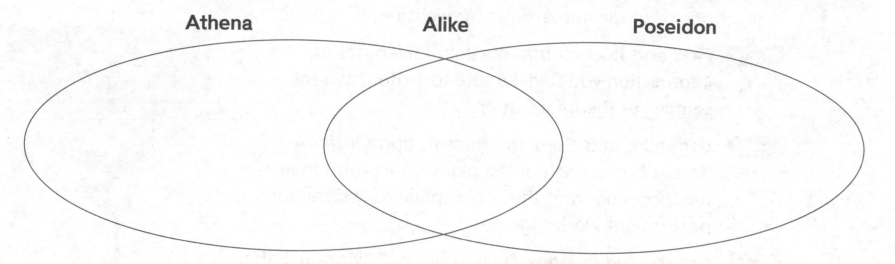

Athena   Alike   Poseidon

Write The author uses stage directions and dialogue to

show _____

_____

CHECK IN 1 2 3 4

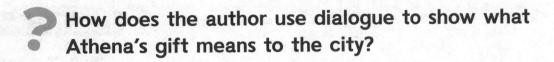

? **How does the author use dialogue to show what Athena's gift means to the city?**

Talk About It Reread pages 522–523. Discuss what Athena sings and what the citizens say about her gift.

Cite Text Evidence Write text evidence that shows why the citizens appreciate, or are thankful for, Athena's gift.

Athena	Citizens

Write The author uses dialogue to show that _____

_____

Quick Tip

In a drama, actors perform the actions and dialogue of the characters. Stage directions and illustrations show the setting. As you reread, think about how these modes work together as ways to tell a story.

Evaluate Information

The character Athena speaks and sings her lines. How does watching and listening to the character help you understand this part of the story?

CHECK IN 1 2 3 4

? **Why is the drama, or play, organized in 3 scenes?**

COLLABORATE

Talk About It Talk about the conflict between Athena and Poseidon and how this problem is solved, or resolved.

Cite Text Evidence Write a brief description of the main event in each scene. Include the conflict and resolution.

Scene 1

```
[                                              ]
```

Scene 2

```
[                                              ]
```

Scene 3

```
[                                              ]
```

Write The author organizes the drama in 3 scenes to show

_____

_____

CHECK IN 1 2 3 4

Respond to Reading

Talk about the prompt below. Use your notes and text evidence to support your response.

How does the behavior of the characters, or how they act and what they say, show that Athena should be patron?

_____

_____

_____

_____

_____

_____

_____

Quick Tip

Use these sentence starters to help you organize your text evidence.

In Scene 1, Poseidon shouts...

During the contest...

At the end of the myth...

CHECK IN ⟩ 1 ⟩ 2 ⟩ 3 ⟩ 4 ⟩

Poseidon's Gift

Poseidon, the god of the sea, cared little about the ways of people. Human beings lived in cities on land. The sea with its crashing waves and salty spray was Poseidon's home and only true interest. Then one day, a young city caught his eye. He marveled at its citizens working away in shops. In the fields, farmers planted crops and tended sheep. The people were as busy as the bees.

Literature Anthology: pages 528–531

Reread the beginning of the story. **Underline** why Poseidon was not interested in what people did.

Why does a young city catch the eye of Poseidon?

_____

_____

COLLABORATE

Discuss what you learn about Poseidon at the beginning of the story?

The people began a tradition.
Before any seagoing trip, they shouted
Poseidon's name so that it might be
heard above the crash of the waves.
And Poseidon always heard them.
The god of the sea learned to care
about the people and keep them safe
whenever they sailed.

Reread the end of the story.
Underline the tradition people start.

How does the reader know that Poseidon cares about this new tradition?

Circle text evidence to support your answer.

_____

_____

_____

_____

COLLABORATE

Discuss how Poseidon's feelings change from the beginning of the story to the end.

? **What do the gifts of Athena and Poseidon explain about the city of Athens?**

Evaluate Information

How do the two gifts change what the people have in the city and what they can do?

Talk About It Read page 531 of the **Literature Anthology.** Discuss how the gifts change the city and the people's way of life.

Cite Text Evidence Write details that describe what happens after Athena and Poseidon give their gifts.

Athena's Gift	Poseidon's Gift

Write The gifts explain how _____

_____

_____

_____

CHECK IN 1 2 3 4

Figurative Language: Similes and Alliteration

Quick Tip

Remember that a simile compares two things using the words *like* or *as*. Alliteration is when more than two words close together begin with the same sounds.

Authors use figurative language, like similes and alliteration, to make writing interesting. Similes can help create pictures in the minds of their readers. Alliteration focuses readers' attention on a section of the text.

FIND TEXT EVIDENCE

On page 529 of the **Literature Anthology,** the author uses a simile to describe the citizens, or people, as being "as busy as bees." Write the simile on page 529 that describes what Poseidon sees in the fields.

_____

_____

Your Turn Reread the last paragraph on page 530. What does the author's use of alliteration help readers focus on?

_____

_____

_____

CHECK IN 1 2 3 4

? **What have you learned about characters in the ancient myths you have read and from the photograph of a Greek bowl, or pottery?**

Talk About It Look at the sculpture and read the caption. Talk with a partner about the ancient Greek God Helios.

Text Evidence In the caption, **underline** a detail that tells what Helios did every day. **Circle** the halo in the image that helps identify him as the god of the Sun.

Write The plays I read and the artwork of Helios

help me understand that myths _____

_____

_____

_____

_____

_____

Quick Tip

Use these sentence starters to talk about the characters you have read about.

Athena gave olive trees to the Greeks because...

Poseidon was...

Aster's tears created...

A Greek bowl portrays Helios, the ancient Greek God of the Sun. Every day, he drove his chariot across the sky from east to west providing sunlight to the world.

CHECK IN 1 > 2 > 3 > 4

My Goal I know about what myths help us understand.

Write a Journal Entry

Think about the characters in the myths you read. How do these characters in mythology teach us lessons about real life?

1. Look at your Build Knowledge notes in your reader's notebook.

2. Write a journal entry about characters from three of the stories you read. Explain how you feel about the lessons they learned.

3. Include some of the new words you learned. Remember to use evidence from three texts to support your ideas.

Think about what you learned in this text set. Fill in the bars on page 37.

Build Knowledge

Build Vocabulary

Write new words you learned about where imagination can take us. Draw lines and circles for the words you write.

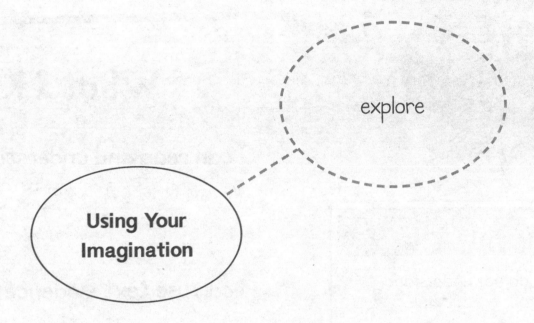

explore

Using Your Imagination

Go online to **my.mheducation.com** and read the "Set Your Imagination Free" Blast. Think about how you can spark your imagination. Then blast back your response.

Think about what you already know. Fill in the bars. We all do better with practice.

Key

1 =	I do not understand.
2 =	I understand but need more practice.
3 =	I understand.
4 =	I understand and can teach someone.

What I Know Now

I can read and understand poetry.

1 > 2 > 3 > 4

I can use text evidence to respond to poetry.

1 > 2 > 3 > 4

I know about where our imaginations can take us.

1 > 2 > 3 > 4

STOP You will come back to the next page later.

Think about what you learned.
Fill in the bars. Good job!

What I Learned

I can read and understand poetry.

1 > 2 > 3 > 4

I can use text evidence to respond to poetry.

1 > 2 > 3 > 4

I know about where our imaginations can take us.

1 > 2 > 3 > 4

My Goal — I can read and understand poetry.

TAKE NOTES
As you read, write down interesting words and important details.

_____

_____

_____

_____

_____

_____

_____

_____

A Box of Crayons

A box of crayons is the sun
on a dreary, rainy day.
You can draw a hot air balloon
and travel far far away.

You can draw a beach
and play in the silky sand.
You can draw a drum
and play in a marching band.

With crayons you can always create
something exciting, something great!

— by Isaiah Nowels

Essential Question

Where can your imagination take you?

Read how poems share ideas and creativity.

What Story Is This ?

None of us are us today,
We're putting on a play.

"Knock, knock, knock! Someone's there!"
That's the wolf, my friend Claire.

"Not by the hair of my chinny-chin chin!"
Julie, a little pig, says with a grin.

Joseph and Pat are pigs as well.
They run to Claire's house and ring the bell.
Do you remember this story's name?

If so, you've won this guessing game!

— by Trevor Reynolds

FIND TEXT EVIDENCE

`Read`
Page 64
Stanzas

Look back at the second stanza, or group of lines. **Underline** what the speaker says you can do with crayons.

Page 65
Character Perspective

Why does the speaker say, "None of us are us today"?

_____

_____

Circle who plays the different parts of the play.

`Reread`
Author's Craft

Why is "What Story Is This?" a good title for this poem?

FIND TEXT EVIDENCE 🔍

Read

Lines 1–4

Character Perspective

Circle the word the speaker uses to describe her ticket. Where can it take her?

_____

_____

_____

Lines 5-8

Stanzas

Underline the lines the poet indents in the second stanza.

Reread

Author's Craft

How does the poet use language to help you use your imagination?

The Ticket

I have a special ticket
    That takes me anywhere,
To oceans deep, the dazzling stars,
    A mighty lion's lair.

I've been to a volcano,
    Which is like a boiling pot,
I even rode a camel,
    Through the desert, burning hot.

I've shivered in the North Pole,
    At 43 below,
And built myself a cozy igloo,
    Out of blocks of snow.

I've met a great inventor,
    And helped him to create,
A baseball playing robot,
    That slides into home plate.

My journeys take just seconds,
    I simply close my eyes,
And I'm a rocket sleek and silver,
    Speeding through the skies.

What's that? You'd like to join me?
    Here's all you have to do:
Use your imagination,
    And you'll soon go places, too!

— by Constance Keremes

Make Connections

Which poem reminds you of fun places or things you have created in your imagination?

FIND TEXT EVIDENCE 🔍

Read

Lines 13–16

Rhyme Scheme

Circle the lines that rhyme in the fourth stanza. Write the rhyming words.

Lines 17–20

Metaphor

Underline what the speaker can be when she closes her eyes. What does she compare herself to?

Reread

Author's Craft

How does the poet express her message at the end of the poem?

Vocabulary

Talk with a partner about each word. Then answer the questions.

create

The artist will **create** a painting.

What can you create with clay?

_____

_____

_____

dazzling

The city lights looked **dazzling** at night.

What is something that looks dazzling?

_____

_____

Interesting Words In your reader's notebook, write a definition of an interesting word you found in a poem.

imagination

Ellie uses **imagination** when she draws.

How do you use your imagination?

_____

_____

seconds

It takes **seconds** to run across the gym.

About how many seconds does it take to write your name?

_____

_____

Poetry Words

beats

The **beats** of a poem are the syllables that make rhythm in a line of poetry.

How many beats are in your first and last name?

_____

_____

message

The poet shared her **message** about using your imagination.

What is the message in a poem you enjoy?

_____

_____

metaphor

"I'm a swan" is a **metaphor** because it compares two unlike things.

Use a metaphor to describe yourself.

_____

_____

repeated lines

Sometimes poets use **repeated lines**. They include the same line at least twice in a poem.

Why might a poet use repeated lines?

_____

_____

Metaphors

A metaphor compares two different things. It does not use the words *like* or *as*.

FIND TEXT EVIDENCE

In "A Box of Crayons," the speaker compares a box of crayons to the sun. The metaphor is "A box of crayons is the sun on a dreary, rainy day."

A box of crayons is the sun
on a dreary, rainy day.
You can draw a hot air balloon
and travel far far away.

Your Turn Complete the sentence to create a metaphor.

The runner is a _____ as he speeds by.

In "The Ticket," the poet compares imagination to a special ticket. Why does the poet use this metaphor? Write your answer in your reader's notebook.

CHECK IN 1 2 3 4

Rhyme Scheme

Words that rhyme begin with different sounds but end with the same sounds. Poets use patterns of rhyming lines to create a rhyme scheme that gives poems feeling.

 FIND TEXT EVIDENCE

As I read "What Story Is This?" aloud, I can hear the rhymes. The rhyme scheme gives the poem a light, cheerful feeling. Rhyming lines also help the poem sound like a song.

Page 65

None of us are us today,
We're putting on a play.

The first and second lines rhyme because the last words rhyme. The rhyming lines make the poem fun to read aloud.

 Your Turn Reread "A Box of Crayons" on page 64 aloud. Mark capital letters after the lines that rhyme. Then write the letters in a row to show the rhyme scheme.

COLLABORATE

_____

_____

 Quick Tip
As you read poems, listen to the last word in each line. This will help you identify the lines that rhyme in the poem.

CHECK IN ⟩ 1 ⟩ 2 ⟩ 3 ⟩ 4 ⟩

Stanzas

A rhyming poem has words with the same sound at the end of certain lines. It has regular, repeating rhythm. Often a rhyming poem is organized in groups of lines called stanzas.

Readers to Writers

A stanza can be a way to organize ideas in your poem. You can group lines that tell about one idea in each stanza.

🔍 **FIND TEXT EVIDENCE**

I can tell that "A Box of Crayons" is a rhyming poem because it has pairs of words that rhyme in each stanza.

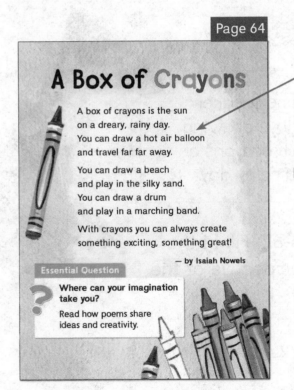

Page 64

A Box of Crayons

A box of crayons is the sun
on a dreary, rainy day.
You can draw a hot air balloon
and travel far far away.

You can draw a beach
and play in the silky sand.
You can draw a drum
and play in a marching band.

With crayons you can always create
something exciting, something great!

— by Isaiah Nowels

Essential Question

? Where can your imagination take you?

Read how poems share ideas and creativity.

A **stanza** is a group of lines, or section, in a poem. In the first stanza, line 2 and line 4 end with rhyming words.

COLLABORATE

Your Turn Reread "The Ticket" on pages 66–67. Discuss how the poet groups lines into stanzas. What lines rhyme in each stanza?

_____

_____

_____

_____

CHECK IN ⟩ 1 ⟩ 2 ⟩ 3 ⟩ 4 ⟩

Character Perspective

The way a speaker, or charcter, in a poem feels about something is his or her perspective.

 FIND TEXT EVIDENCE

When I read "A Box of Crayons" on page 64, I ask myself about the character's perspective, or the speaker's feelings.

Quick Tip

Taking notes on what the speaker says or feels about something in the poem will help you to identify his or her point of view.

Character	Clue	Perspective
speaker	A box of crayons is the sun / on a dreary, rainy day.	The speaker enjoys drawing with crayons on a rainy day.

 Your Turn Reread "The Ticket" on pages 66-67. Fill in the graphic organizer to help you identify the perspective of the character, or speaker, in the poem.

CHECK IN 1 2 3 4

Character	Clue	Perspective
speaker	A box of crayons is the sun / on a dreary, rainy day.	The speaker enjoys drawing with crayons on a rainy day.

I can use text evidence to respond to poetry.

Respond to Reading

COLLABORATE

Talk about the prompt below. Use your notes and text evidence to support your answer.

How do all the poets show how they feel about imagination?

_____

_____

_____

_____

_____

_____

_____

_____

Quick Tip

Use these sentence starters to help you organize your text evidence.

The poet uses...

The speaker in "A Box of Crayons"...

In "What Story Is This?"...

In "The Ticket"...

Grammar Connections

Remember to capitalize important words when you write the title of a poem, and remember to put the title in quotes. For example: "A Box of Crayons."

CHECK IN   1   2   3   4

Authors and Artists

COLLABORATE

With a partner, create an oral report about an author or artist from your state. Follow the research process to create your oral report.

Step 1 **Set a Goal** Find an author or artist from your state that you would like to learn more about. Choose one of this person's poems, stories, songs, or pieces of art to share.

Write your topic: _____

Step 2 **Identify Sources** Write questions you want to answer in your research. Use audio such as recorded music or an interview. Use visuals such as a video clip or slide presentation.

Step 3 **Find and Record Information** Be sure to write down any information you find in your own words. Also write down the sources of the information you find.

Step 4 **Organize and Combine Information** As you organize information, be sure to include audio and visuals in your presentation.

Step 5 **Create and Present** Take turns presenting your oral report to the class. Be sure you have the equipment you may need for your presentation.

CHECK IN ▶ 1 ⟩ 2 ⟩ 3 ⟩ 4 ⟩

wavebreakmedia/Shutterstock

Literature Anthology:
pages 532–535

I've Got This Covered

? How does the poet use the perspective of a book cover to express her feelings about reading?

Talk About It Reread "I've Got This Covered" on page 533. Discuss the book cover's perspective, or what it is thinking.

Cite Text Evidence What details show the perspective of the book cover? Write text evidence in the chart.

Make Inferences

What clues helped you figure out that the speaker is a book cover?

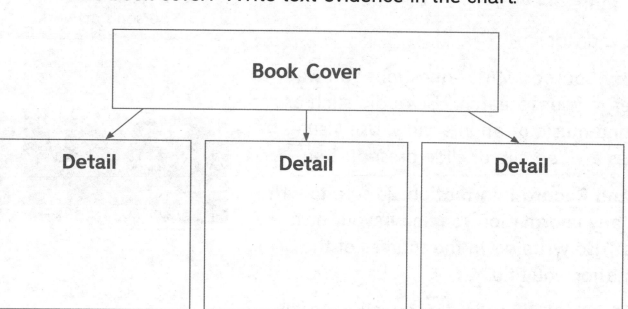

Book Cover

Detail	Detail	Detail

Write The poet uses the perspective of _____

_____

_____

CHECK IN 1 2 3 4

Eating While Reading

 How does the poet use descriptive language to show how he feels about eating and reading?

Talk About It Reread the poem on page 534. Talk about the descriptions in the speaker's questions.

Cite Text Evidence What details show how the poet feels about eating and reading? Write the text evidence.

Eating	Reading

Write The poet uses descriptive language to show how he

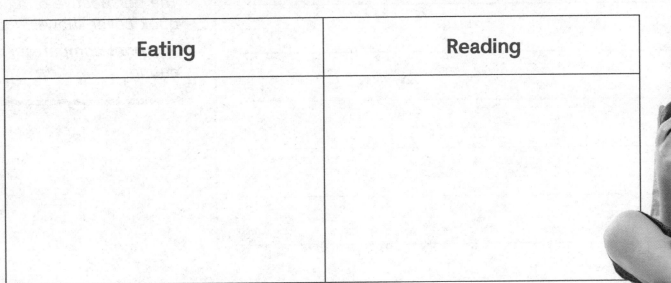

Combine Information
What details about eating does the speaker describe as "This sweet dance/ On the tongue"?

CHECK IN 1 2 3 4

Rido/Shutterstock

Respond to Reading

My Goal **I can use text evidence to respond to poetry.**

COLLABORATE

Discuss the prompt below. Use your notes and text evidence to support your response.

How do the poets help you to understand different ways people enjoy reading?

_____

_____

_____

_____

_____

_____

_____

Quick Tip

Use these sentence starters to organize your text evidence.

The poet calls his books...

The perspective of a book cover shows...

The poet compares eating...

CHECK IN ▶ 1 〉 2 〉 3 〉 4 〉

Clay Play

? **How does the poet use descriptive language to express her point of view?**

Literature Anthology: pages 536–537

Talk About It Reread "Clay Play" on page 536. Talk about what the poet says about how to play with clay.

Cite Text Evidence The poet uses strong verbs as descriptive words. Write the phrases with strong verbs.

Quick Tip

The strong verbs the poet uses will help you visualize playing with clay.

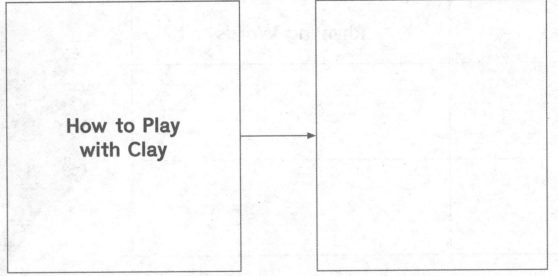

How to Play with Clay

Write The poet uses descriptive words to help me

understand _____

_____

CHECK IN 1 2 3 4

Crayons

? **How does the poet of "Crayons" use rhyme to make the poem interesting to read?**

Talk About It Reread page 537. Talk about where the lines rhyme and how the rhymes make you feel.

Cite Text Evidence In the chart, write the number of the lines that rhyme. Write the rhyming words in these lines.

Rhyming Lines	Rhyming Words
Lines 2 and 4	

Write The rhyming lines make the poem interesting

_____

_____

Quick Tip

Remember to pause at the end of each line in a poem. This will also help you to hear the rhyming words in a poem.

CHECK IN 1 2 3 4

Rhythm and Rhyme

Rhythm is a pattern of beats in a poem. Rhythm can make a poem sound like a song and interesting or fun to read.

Poets use repetition to add rhythm. Poets also use rhyming lines and indent lines to add rhythm to a poem.

 FIND TEXT EVIDENCE

Reread the first stanza of "Clay Play" on page 536. Each line has short phrases with the pronoun *it*. Listen to the rhythm in the first stanza as you read aloud. Remember to pause for each comma.

 Your Turn Reread the rest of the poem aloud with your partner. Talk about how the rhythm changes in the second and third stanzas. In these two stanzas, what lines does the author indent and rhyme?

_____

_____

_____

Don't be afraid to play with language when you write a rhyming poem. Read the words out loud to hear how they sound together. Try different words to hear how they change the rhythm. Repeat some words or phrases and see how it sounds.

? How do the painter and the poets of "I've Got This Covered" and "Clay Play" use their imaginations to help you think in new ways?

Talk About It Talk about what you see in the painting. How does it open your imagination?

Cite Text Evidence In the caption, **underline** how the painter uses imagination in the painting. Think about why the painter wants to show art this way.

Write The poets and the painter use their imaginations

to help me _____

_____

_____

_____

_____

_____

In this painting, the ocean waves in a picture break out of their frame and flow into the real world.

Quick Tip

Talk about the painting and the poems using these sentence starters.

The painting of the ocean…

The speaker in "I've Got This Covered" made me think about books as…

"Clay Play" gave me new ideas about…

CHECK IN 1 2 3 4

My Goal I know about where imagination can take us.

Write a Poem

Think about the topics in the poems you read. How do the poets use their imagination in each poem? Write a poem that describes how you enjoy using your imagination.

1 Look at your Build Knowledge notes in your reader's notebook.

2 In your poem, write about a time you used your imagination to create or discover something new. Then make connections with three poems you read by describing how everyone can use their imaginations.

3 Include some of the new words you learned. Remember to use evidence from three of the poems you read to support your ideas.

Think about what you learned in this text set. Fill in the bars on page 63.

Think about what you already know. Fill in the bars. Now let's get started!

Key
1 = I do not understand.
2 = I understand but need more practice.
3 = I understand.
4 = I understand and can teach someone.

What I Know Now

I can write an expository essay.

1 〉 2 〉 3 〉 4

I can combine information from three sources.

1 〉 2 〉 3 〉 4

STOP You will come back to the next page later.

Think about what you learned. Fill in the bars. The more you write, the more you'll improve.

What I Learned

I can write an expository essay.

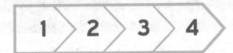

I can combine information from three sources.

1 2 3 4

WRITING

WRITE TO SOURCES

You will answer an expository writing prompt using sources and a rubric.

ANALYZE THE RUBRIC

A rubric tells you what to include in your writing.

Purpose, Focus, and Organization

Read the fifth bullet. What is at the beginning of an essay? What is at the end?

_____

_____

Evidence and Elaboration

Read the third bullet. **Circle** the different types of details to use in an essay.

Read the fourth bullet. **Underline** what precise language does.

Valentain Jevee/Shutterstock

Expository Writing Rubric

Purpose, Focus, and Organization • Score 4

- Stays focused on purpose, audience, and task
- **States the central idea, or main idea**
- Connects ideas with transitional words
- Presents ideas in a logical order
- Begins with an introduction and ends with a conclusion that sums up the topic

Evidence and Elaboration • Score 4

- Supports the central idea with facts and details
- Includes relevant evidence, or supporting details, from the sources
- Uses elaborative techniques, such as examples, definitions, and quotations
- Expresses ideas clearly with precise language
- Uses academic vocabulary to explain the topic
- Has different sentence types and lengths

Turn to page 130 for the complete Expository Writing Rubric.

Central Idea

Stating the Central Idea The central idea is the writer's main point, or big idea. It tells the focus of the essay, or what it is about. State the central idea at the beginning of the essay. Read the introduction to an essay below.

> Farms near you grow delicious fruits and vegetables. Local produce is sold in supermarkets. You can even get food straight from local farmers. **Local produce tastes good and is good for you. Buying it also helps others in the community**. Someday I want to own a farm.

Audience
Your readers may be classmates or others who don't know much about your topic. Think about how to make the information in your essay interesting and easy to understand.

The central idea is highlighted. What does it tell about the focus of the essay?

_____

_____

Supporting Details Unimportant details do not help the reader understand the topic or central idea. Reread the paragraph above. Cross out the unimportant detail.

ANALYZE THE STUDENT MODEL

Paragraphs 1–2

Read the highlighted central idea. Tom states three reasons to buy local produce. What is the first?

_____

_____

Underline two details that explain why people enjoy eating local produce.

Paragraph 3

Draw a box around the transitional word that shows another reason why people want local produce.

Circle why people want to know about their food.

Student Model: Expository Essay

Tom responded to the writing prompt: *Write an expository essay that explains why families want to buy food from local farms*. Read Tom's essay below.

1   Farms near you grow delicious fruits and vegetables. Local produce is sold in supermarkets. You can even get food straight from local farmers. Local produce tastes good and is good for you. Buying it also helps others in the community.

2   First, people buy local produce because it is fresh. In "The Farmer's Market," the author explains why local produce is always fresh. It does not have to travel far to stores. It is picked soon before you can eat it. The author of "A CSA" states that "fruit and vegetables taste best when they are fresh." In addition, local farms give us more choices of fruits and vegetables to enjoy.

3   Second, people want to know about the food they eat. They want to know it is good for their families.

Titus Group/Shutterstock; Nata Studio/Shutterstock

Local farmers explain how they grow their food. You can even talk to farmers at a farmer's market. The author of "Local Foods" explains why local produce is good for you. It can add different nutrients to your meals. Nutrients help people stay healthy.

4   Last, people want to support local farmers. In "The Farmer's Market," the author tells how farms are businesses. Buying from local farms helps the farmers earn money for their families. In a group called a CSA, the members pay the salary of farmers. A salary is money someone earns from work.

5   People want food that tastes good and keeps them healthy. People also care about farmers. One author explains how families "want to feel a connection to the people who grow their food." For these reasons, some families like to buy from local farmers.

Paragraph 3
Circle evidence from "Local Foods" that tells why local produce is good for you.

Paragraph 4
What did Tom explain about buying from local farms?

_____

_____

_____

Draw a box around the definition of the word *salary*.

Paragraph 5
Underline the quotation that tells more about why people buy from local farms.

Apply the Rubric

With a partner, use the rubric on page 86 to discuss why Tom scored 10 points on his essay.

Analyze the Prompt

Writing Prompt

Write an expository essay that explains why agriculture, or farming, is an important business in Florida.

Purpose, Audience, and Task Reread the writing prompt.

What is your purpose for writing? My purpose is to _____

_____

Who will your audience be? My audience will be _____

_____

What type of writing is the prompt asking for? _____

_____

Set a Purpose for Reading Sources Asking questions about farming in Florida will help you figure out your purpose for reading. Write a question before reading the passages.

_____

_____

_____

Read the following passage set.

Meet Cara from South Florida

1   Like most of us, you probably buy your food in a store. And, if you're lucky, you might also shop at a farmer's market. Did you ever think about the fact that kids help grow some of that food?

2   **In Florida's warm climate, Cara's family raises vegetables and lychees.** Lychee trees grow only in warm climates. They produce fruit slightly larger than grapes and much sweeter. Their seeds can be dried and sold as lychee nuts.

3   Cara's family can grow four vegetable crops per year on the same land. These include tomatoes and corn in the winter, beans in the summer, and okra in the fall. Her family hires workers to help plant, fertilize, spray, and harvest.

4   Eight-year-old Cara likes being in the fields and orchard with her dad. She also helps with a garden at school and enjoys dance lessons.

EXPOSITORY ESSAY

FIND TEXT EVIDENCE 🔍

Paragraphs 1–2
Read the highlighted central idea. Why is the climate in Florida important to Cara's family?

_____

_____

Circle a detail that supports the central idea.

Paragraph 3
Draw a box around what the warm climate allows Cara's family to do.

Underline what can grow in South Florida in winter.

Take Notes Paraphrase the central idea of the source and take notes on supporting details.

FIND TEXT EVIDENCE

Paragraph 5

Two details are highlighted. **Underline** the central idea they support.

Paragraph 6

Circle why Florida can grow more tomatoes than any other state.

Why is this important to American consumers?

_____

_____

_____

Paragraph 7

Draw a box around two details that explain why lettuce is grown in Florida.

SOURCE 2

AMERICA'S WINTER SALAD BOWL

5   It's freezing outside! Snow is falling from gray skies. This is winter weather in parts of our country. **But lettuce, tomatoes, and bell peppers for a salad can grow in Florida**. During the cold season, much of the produce Americans eat comes from Florida. **That's why people call our state "America's winter salad bowl."**

6   Juicy tomatoes grow well in warm, sunny weather. The Sunshine State grows more tomatoes than any other. Tomatoes are shipped around the country. Thanks to Florida, American consumers, or shoppers, can buy fresh tomatoes all year long.

7   Lettuce for your salad also grows well in warm weather. One part of Florida has soil that is fertile for growing lettuce. It is called muck soil. There are more than 87 lettuce farms in Florida. Romaine and leafy lettuce are the most common crops on these farms.

8   Bell peppers add flavor and color to any salad. Florida is the second largest producer of bell peppers. But bell peppers don't grow so well in hot weather. They are harvested during cooler months of the year in Florida. When farmers *harvest*, they pick their crops.

9   Vegetables are part of a healthy diet. In the cold season, many Americans depend on their *winter salad bowl*, Florida, for fresh produce.

Florida Fruits and Vegetables in Season

	Jan	Feb	Mar	Apr	May	Jun	Jul	Aug	Sep	Oct	Nov	Dec
Avocado	✓					✓	✓	✓	✓	✓	✓	✓
Bell Pepper	✓	✓	✓	✓	✓						✓	✓
Broccoli	✓	✓	✓									
Cauliflower	✓	✓	✓	✓								✓
Celery	✓	✓	✓	✓	✓							✓
Lettuce	✓	✓	✓	✓								✓
Mushroom	✓	✓	✓	✓	✓	✓	✓	✓	✓	✓	✓	✓
Tomato	✓	✓	✓	✓	✓	✓				✓	✓	✓

Chart

How does the chart show that food is grown all year in Florida?

_____

_____

Paragraph 8

Draw a box around when bell peppers grow well in Florida.

Circle the definition of the content word *harvest*.

Paragraph 9

In the conclusion, **underline** the sentence that restates the central idea.

Take Notes Paraphrase the central idea of the source and give examples of supporting details.

Paragraph 10

Underline why Florida citrus is big business. **Circle** the transitional words that help readers understand that this is the reason why.

Paragraph 11

Read the highlighted details. How do they support that Florida citrus is big business?

_____

_____

_____

Paragraph 12

Underline facts the author gives that tell about Florida orange juice.

The Business of Citrus

10   A sweet, juicy orange is a citrus fruit. A grapefruit is another type of citrus fruit. It tastes sweet and tangy. Citrus trees grow well in the warm sun. For this reason, citrus fruit has become big business in Florida. People all over the world buy Florida citrus fruit and fruit juices.

11   Florida produces more grapefruits than any other state. **The fruit is sent by trains, ships, or trucks to stores all over our country. Florida also exports more grapefruits than any other place in the world.** To _export_ means to sell to a different country. Many Florida grapefruits are sold thousands of miles away to Asia and Europe.

12   Do you know the state fruit of Florida? Here's a hint: it's _orange_! Florida produces the most oranges in the United States. About 90 percent of these oranges are used for juice. It's not surprising that most of the orange juice we Americans drink comes from Florida.

13 Florida is the leading state in the citrus industry, or business. It has been the leader for over 100 years. This has created many jobs in Florida. It also generates, or makes, money for the state. This money can be used for Florida's schools and highways.

14 Florida oranges and grapefruits are famous for being fresh and delicious. People all around the world eat them every day. The big business of citrus has benefited the state of Florida.

Paragraph 13

Circle two benefits of the citrus industry to people in Florida.

What can the state do with money that comes from the citrus industry?

_____

_____

_____

Paragraph 14

Underline a statement that tells how the author feels about the citrus industry in Florida.

Take Notes Paraphrase the central idea of the source and give examples of supporting details.

My Goal I can combine information from three sources.

TAKE NOTES

Read the writing prompt below. Use the three sources, your notes, and the graphic organizer to plan a response.

Writing Prompt *Write an expository essay that explains why agriculture, or farming, is an important business in Florida.*

Combine Information

Review evidence recorded from the sources. How does the information show agriculture is important to people in Florida and in other places? Discuss your ideas with a partner.

CHECK IN 1 2 3 4

Plan: Organize Ideas

Central Idea	Supporting Ideas
The climate, or weather, makes farming an important business in Florida.	Florida is warm and sunny.

Relevant Evidence

Source 1	Source 2	Source 3
Cara's family can grow lychee trees in warm climate.	Produce, such as lettuce and tomatoes, grow well in sunshine and warmth.	Citrus trees grow well in warm and sunny climate.

Valentain Jevee/Shutterstock

Draft: Elaborative Techniques

Supporting Details Elaborative techniques are ways to add supporting details, or relevant evidence, from sources. Define an important word, quote an author's exact words, or paraphrase an example from the source.

In the sentence below, a writer quotes a fact from paragraph 11 on page 94. Reread paragraph 11, and then elaborate on the fact by writing a definition and an example in your own words.

Quick Tip

Remember, *elaborate* means to give more details or to explain more fully. Elaborative techniques are how you support an important point in your essay.

> In Source 3, the author states, "Florida also exports more grapefruits than any other place in the world."

_____

_____

_____

Use your graphic organizer to write your draft in your writer's notebook. Be sure to use elaborative techniques to include relevant evidence. Before you start writing, review the rubric on page 86.

CHECK IN 1 2 3 4

Revise: Peer Conferences

Review a Draft Listen carefully as a partner reads his or her work aloud. Say what you like about the draft. Use these sentence starters to talk about your partner's draft.

This supporting idea is strong because...
I have a question about...
I think you can add details about...

Write one of the suggestions from your partner that you will use in your revision.

✓ Revising Checklist

- [ ] Do I have an introduction?
- [ ] Do I use transitional words?
- [ ] Does it have a conclusion?
- [ ] Did I check my spelling and punctuation?

_____

_____

 Revision Use the Revising Checklist to help you figure out what text you may need to move, elaborate on, or delete. When you finish writing your final draft, use the full rubric on page 130 to score your essay.

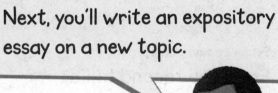
Next, you'll write an expository essay on a new topic.

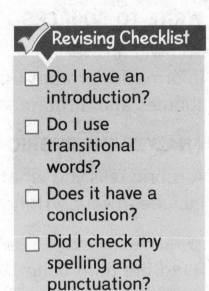

My Score	Purpose, Focus & Organization (4 pts)	Evidence & Elaboration (4 pts)	Conventions (2 pts)	Total (10 pts)

WRITE TO SOURCES

You will answer an informative prompt using sources and a rubric.

ANALYZE THE RUBRIC

A rubric tells you what to include in your writing.

Purpose, Focus, and Organization

Read the third bullet. What do transitional words do?

_____

_____

Evidence and Elaboration

Read the second bullet. **Circle** where relevant evidence about the topic comes from.

Read the fifth bullet. **Underline** what words help readers, or the audience, understand the topic.

Expository Writing Rubric

Purpose, Focus, and Organization • Score 4

- Stays focused on purpose, audience, and task
- States the central idea, or main idea
- Connects ideas with transitional words
- Presents ideas in a logical order
- **Begins with an introduction and ends with a conclusion that sums up the topic**

Evidence and Elaboration • Score 4

- Supports the central idea with facts and details
- Includes relevant evidence, or supporting details, from the sources
- Uses elaborative techniques, such as examples, definitions, and quotations
- Expresses ideas clearly with precise language
- Uses academic vocabulary to explain the topic
- Has different sentence types and lengths

Turn to page 130 for the complete Expository Writing Rubric.

Conclusion

Strong Ending A conclusion restates the central idea from the introduction. This is a way to summarize the main points of the essay. Writers sometimes also include an interesting idea in the conclusion. Read the conclusion below. The highlighted sentences restate the central idea.

Audience

The conclusion should help your readers remember what you want them to learn from your essay. You may add an interesting idea about the essay's topic that you want your readers to think more about.

> **Kids are learning more about clean energy. They are using what they know to create new ways to make things work.** Imagine a world without pollution. Learn about clean energy and it might come true.

What does the writer tell readers to imagine? **Circle** the sentence in the conclusion that tells you. What idea does the writer want readers to think more about?

_____

_____

_____

CHECK IN 1 2 3 4

(bkgd) Valentain Jevee/Shutterstock

Irene responded to the writing prompt: *Write an expository essay that describes how kids learned more about sources of clean energy.* Read Irene's essay below.

ANALYZE THE STUDENT MODEL

Paragraph 1

How are some kids learning about clean energy?

_____

_____

Paragraph 2

Draw a box around the quotation that describes what the kids created.

Circle the reason it does not pollute the air. What words signal, or show, that this is the reason why?

_____

Paragraph 3

Underline evidence from "Solar Racers" that tells what other students made.

1   Imagine living in a world without pollution. That might mean using new kinds of energy to make things work. One kind of clean energy is solar power. It is good for our planet. Some kids are learning about clean energy by creating new ways to make things go.

2   High school kids in Arizona wanted to make a car that doesn't pollute. In an article about the school's science club, the author tells about how the students turned "a regular pickup truck into a clean energy truck." They learned how to use solar energy and water to power an engine. The truck does not run on gasoline. As a result, it does not pollute the air.

3   Other kids built model cars that run on solar power. The students from the source called "Solar Racers"

learned about solar cells. They learned about how the solar cells turn light from the Sun into electricity. The kids attached the solar cells to the cars. They figured out how to make sure the cars got enough power from the Sun. They also learned how to work together. They tested their cars and shared ideas to make sure their cars went fast.

4   Another source of clean energy is people. The diagram in "Pedal Power" shows how the rear wheel of a bicycle can produce electricity. Students learned that the power can be saved in a battery. Then computers and small appliances like fans can run on the battery. What a fun and creative way to make things work!

5   Kids are learning more about clean energy. They are using what they know to create new ways to make things work. Imagine a world without pollution. Learn about clean energy and it might come true.

EXPOSITORY ESSAY

Paragraph 3

Circle what these kids learned about solar cells.

Draw a box around why they shared ideas.

Paragraph 4

How does Irene use the diagram in "Pedal Power"?

_____

_____

_____

Paragraph 5

The highlighted sentences restate the central idea. **Underline** the central idea in paragraph 1.

Apply the Rubric

With a partner, use the rubric on page 100 to discuss why Irene scored 10 points on her essay.

Analyze the Prompt

Writing Prompt

Write an expository essay that explains how three inventors improved the ways people used electricity.

Purpose, Audience, and Task Reread the writing prompt. What is your purpose for writing? My purpose is to _____

_____

Who will your audience be? My audience will be _____

_____

What type of writing is the prompt asking for? _____

_____

Set a Purpose for Reading Sources Asking questions about what you want to learn about the inventors will help you figure out your purpose for reading. Write a question you want to answer by reading the passages.

_____

_____

Read the following passage set.

Otis Boykin

1   Have you ever seen a television from the 1950s? **Electronic devices have improved over the years. Otis Boykin was an African-American inventor who helped make this possible.**

2   Boykin worked in electronics. He became interested in resistors. A resistor controls the flow of electricity. It allows only a safe amount to run a device. In the 1950s, resistors did not work well. Boykin worked to improve them.

3   In 1959, Boykin got a patent for a new resistor. Inventors get patents so others cannot use their ideas without permission. Then, he improved the resistor again. It made devices more reliable and last longer. It also made them more affordable.

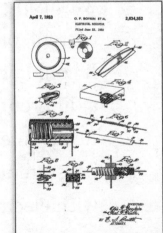

4   Otis Boykin would get 26 patents for his inventions. But his resistor helped make many more devices better, safer, and cheap enough for many people to buy.

Source: United States Patent and Trademark Office, www.uspto.gov

---

EXPOSITORY ESSAY

FIND TEXT EVIDENCE

Paragraph 1
Read the highlighted central idea. What did Otis Boykin help improve?

_____

_____

Paragraph 2
Circle what resistors do in electronic devices.

Draw a box around what Boykin worked to do.

Paragraphs 3 and 4
Underline evidence that tells how Boykin's invention made resistors better.

Take Notes Paraphrase the central idea and give examples of supporting details.

FIND TEXT EVIDENCE

Paragraph 5

What did Tesla use to solve problems?

_____

_____

What did he help bring to people's everyday lives?

_____

_____

Paragraph 6

Underline evidence that tells about problems with Edison's system.

Draw a box around why Tesla's system was better.

Read the idea highlighted in the beginning of paragraph 6. **Circle** what Tesla's AC system still does today.

SOURCE 2

Nikola Tesla

5   Nikola Tesla was born in Europe in 1856. Tesla loved science and using his imagination to solve problems. He came to America to work as an inventor. During his lifetime, Tesla got hundreds of patents for his creations. Much of Tesla's important work was with energy. He worked to bring electricity to people's everyday lives.

6   **Tesla's work helped people to produce and get power.** Another inventor named Thomas Edison was using an electrical system called direct current, or DC, to power lights. This was expensive. It could not send power long distances. Tesla used a different system called alternate current, or AC. It was safer and cheaper. In 1893, Tesla showed his system in Chicago. It still supplies America with electric power today.

7   Niagara Falls is the biggest waterfall in North America. One of Tesla's dreams was to harness, or use, the power of Niagara Falls. In 1895, his dream came true. He created the first modern power plant. It was a hydroelectric plant. It turned energy from moving water into electricity. The station supplied electricity to the city of Buffalo. Tesla's power plant made him famous.

8   Tesla visualized, or pictured, how to improve technology. This helped him to create inventions that changed how people could produce and use electricity. Tesla used his imagination to help him solve problems. He urged everyone to use their imagination to find solutions in their work.

Nikola Tesla with an invention called a Tesla coil

John Parrot/Stocktrek Images/Getty Images

FIND TEXT EVIDENCE 🔍

Paragraph 7
What did Tesla create? Where was it?

_____

_____

_____

Underline how it produced power and what it supplied.

Paragraph 8
Why did Tesla urge others to use their imagination?

_____

_____

_____

Take Notes Paraphrase how Tesla helped people to produce and get power. Give examples of supporting details.

FIND TEXT EVIDENCE 🔍

Paragraph 9

What did Lewis Latimer work hard to do?

_____

_____

Paragraph 10

Underline what Lewis made early in his career and what the drawings were used for.

Circle the author's definition of the word *patent*.

Paragraph 11

Read the highlighted supporting detail. Why did Lewis Latimer need to improve Edison's light bulb?

_____

_____

SOURCE 3

Lewis Latimer

9   Lewis Latimer overcame many challenges as a young person. His family was enslaved when he was born. During the Civil War, Lewis joined the navy. He was only 16. After the war, Lewis worked hard to become a great inventor.

10   Early in his career, Lewis worked at a law firm. He made drawings of inventions that showed how they worked. These drawings were used to apply for patents. A patent protects an inventor's ideas from being used by others. Lewis helped get a patent for the invention of the telephone.

11   It was an exciting time for invention. Thomas Edison had invented a new light bulb. But these bulbs were expensive and didn't last long. Latimer found a way to improve their technology. He added a special envelope. He made other improvements. **His inventions made light bulbs cheaper and last longer. Now more people could buy them.**

12   Later, Latimer worked with Edison. He joined a group of inventors called the Edison Pioneers. But Latimer also worked to help others. He worked for the civil rights of African Americans. He also gave English lessons to immigrants and helped young inventors. Lewis Latimer wanted others to be successful. He never forgot the challenges he faced as a young person.

13   People benefited from Latimer's work with electricity. His inventions helped light up cities. But Latimer helped make people's lives brighter too.

Latimer joins the navy.
1864

Latimer joins the Edison Pioneers.
1918

1848
Lewis Latimer is born.

1881
Latimer improves Edison's light bulb.

1928
Lewis Latimer dies.

FLHC 57/Alamy Stock Photo

EXPOSITORY ESSAY

FIND TEXT EVIDENCE 🔍

Paragraph 12
Underline details that explain how Lewis Latimer helped others.

Paragraph 13
Circle one way his inventions benefited, or helped, people.

Timeline
What year did Lewis Latimer improve Edison's invention?

_____

_____

Take Notes Paraphrase the main focus of each paragraph. Give examples of supporting details.

WRITING

My Goal I can combine informatation from three sources.

TAKE NOTES

Read the writing prompt below. Use the three sources, your notes, and the graphic organizer to plan a response.

Writing Prompt *Write an informative essay that explains how three inventors improved the ways people used electricity.*

Combine Information

Review the evidence recorded from each source. How does the information show how the inventors helped people to use electricity? Discuss your ideas with a partner.

CHECK IN 1 2 3 4

110 Unit 6 • Expository Writing

Central Idea	Supporting Ideas
The inventors fixed problems people once had with electricity and electronic devices.	The inventors wanted to make something work better.

Relevant Evidence

Source 1	Source 2	Source 3
The resistors in devices did not work well.	Edison's system was expensive. It could not send power long distances.	Edison's light bulb did not last long. It was expensive.

(bkgd) Valentain Jevee/Shutterstock

Draft: Academic Vocabulary

Content Words When you write, use words from the sources that will help readers understand the topic. Explain their meanings with definitions and examples. Read the sentences below.

> He worked in |electronics.| He became interested in resistors. A resistor controls the flow of electricity.

Read the content word in the box above. **Circle** another content word in the text. Then **underline** the sentence that tells what it means.

Explain the meaning of *electronics*. A dictionary can help you define the word or give examples.

_____

_____

_____

 Use your graphic organizer to write your draft in your writer's notebook. Before you start writing, review the rubric on page 100. Remember to help your audience understand important words about your topic.

CHECK IN ▷ 1 ▷ 2 ▷ 3 ▷ 4 ▷

Revise: Peer Conferences

COLLABORATE

Review a Draft Listen carefully as a partner reads his or her work aloud. Say what you like about the draft. Use these sentence starters to talk about your partner's draft.

This introduction is strong because...
I have a question about...
I think you should define this academic word...

Write one of the suggestions from your partner that you will use in your revision.

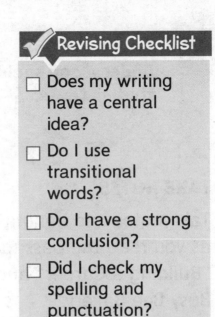

✔ **Revising Checklist**

☐ Does my writing have a central idea?

☐ Do I use transitional words?

☐ Do I have a strong conclusion?

☐ Did I check my spelling and punctuation?

_____

_____

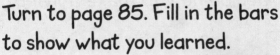
Turn to page 85. Fill in the bars to show what you learned.

Revision Use the Revising Checklist to help you figure out what text you may need to move, elaborate on, or delete. When you finish writing your final draft, use the full rubric on page 130 to score your essay.

	Purpose, Focus & Organization (4 pts)	Evidence & Elaboration (4 pts)	Conventions (2 pts)	Total (10 pts)
My Score				

TAKE NOTES

Take notes and annotate as you read the passages "Building a Career" and "The Busy Bee Bakery."

Look for the answer to this question: *How do people decide how to make a living?*

_____

_____

_____

_____

_____

_____

PASSAGE 1

EXPOSITORY TEXT

BUILDING A CAREER

How do people choose ways to earn money as they get older? Some choose the same jobs their parents chose. Some decide to become something that involves studying for a long time. Others choose several different jobs over the years.

Angie chose to be an architect. Architects plan and design houses, buildings, and other structures. They figure out how much time it will take to build and what it will cost.

When Angie was a kid, she drew houses and buildings. She dreamed of designing buildings where people could live or work. As she got older, she decided to be an architect.

Angie studied to become an architect for many years.

Stockbroker Xtra/Glow Images

Then she started working. Now Angie is saving her money so she can design her own house one day.

Architects often work in offices, but they also travel to construction sites. Some architects work for themselves. The money they make can vary. Having certain skills can help an architect earn more. It also matters where an architect works and for how long.

Angie is happy with her choice. She likes designing buildings. The work is hard but keeps Angie busy and excited. She is also doing a good job of saving her money. Angie is getting closer to creating her own dream home!

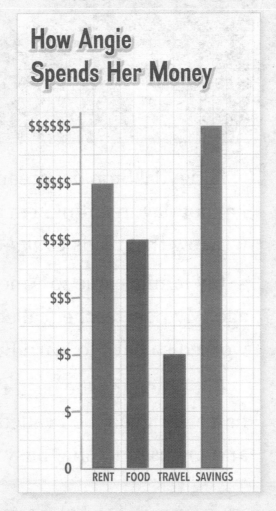

How Angie Spends Her Money

$$$$$$
$$$$$
$$$$
$$$
$$
$
0

RENT   FOOD   TRAVEL   SAVINGS

TAKE NOTES

_____

_____

_____

_____

_____

_____

_____

_____

_____

_____

_____

_____

PASSAGE 2 · HISTORICAL FICTION

THE BUSY BEE BAKERY

"Brigyda! Stop daydreaming!" my mother calls. But I'm not daydreaming. I'm admiring the banner in the window that reads _Grand Opening of The Busy Bee!_

My family came to America from Poland three years ago. My new teacher called me _Busy Bee_ because I worked so hard to learn English.

But I thought she used the letter _b_ because of my name—Brigyda. So I called my brother Milosz, Busy M, and my friend Sofia, Busy S! Later, I learned that a bee is a busy insect that makes honey. My mother bakes delicious honey cakes, so *Busy Bee* is a good name for our bakery!

I thought about the day our family arrived at Ellis Island. We immigrated to have a better life. In my father's bag were carpentry tools. In my mother's bag were recipes.

When we first moved into our tiny apartment, my mother began baking. "To honor our sweet life!" she said. "And to turn strangers into sweet friends!" We delivered honey cakes to everyone on our street.

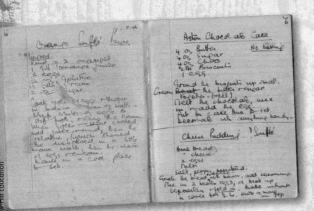

"More!" our new friends said. "We will pay you!" So, my father built a small bakery on the first floor with a long glass case to show off our honey cakes, cream cakes, and fruit tarts. Today, I smile and welcome our new friends coming to buy our tasty, Polish treats!

whitemapExx/Getty Images; McGraw-Hill Education

Compare the Passages

COLLABORATE

Talk About It Reread your notes from "Building a Career" and "The Busy Bee Bakery." What jobs do the people have? Why did they choose them?

Cite Text Evidence Write about what led people to choose and do a job in each passage. Fill in the Venn diagram with details that are similar or different.

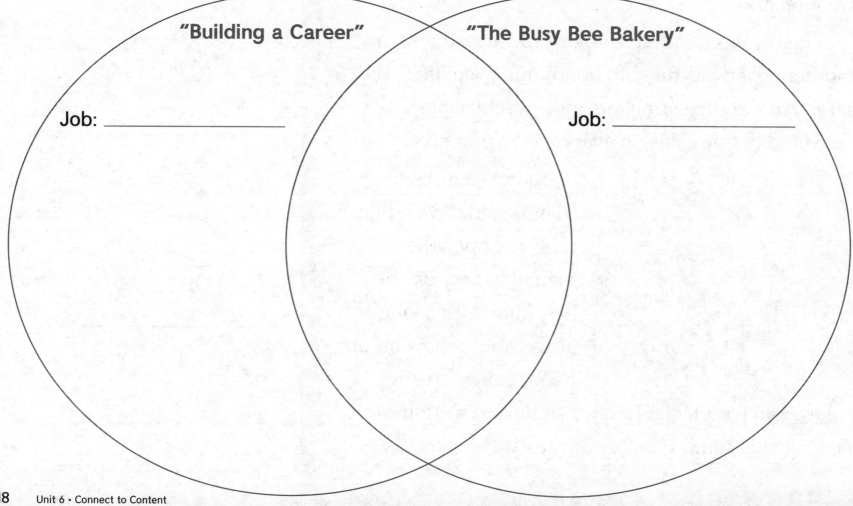

"Building a Career"   "The Busy Bee Bakery"

Job: _____   Job: _____

How do people decide how to make a living?

Talk About It Look at the Venn diagram on page 118. Talk about "Building a Career" and "The Busy Bee Bakery." What led Angie to become an architect and Brigyda's family to open a bakery?

Write When choosing a job, people can think about

_____

_____

_____

_____

_____

_____

Quick Tip

Use these sentence starters to talk about Brigyda's family and about Angie.

When she was a child, Angie...

Angie wanted to...

Brigyda's parents brought...

Both Angie and Brigyda's family...

Combine Information

People have different reasons for choosing jobs. What other reasons can you think of? What reasons do you think are the most important when deciding how to make a living?

CHECK IN 1 2 3 4

Role-Play an Interview

In an interview, you ask questions to find out information. With a partner, write questions a reporter could ask someone from the passages about why they chose their job. Then write answers based on the text.

The reporter will interview: _____

Question 1: _____

Answer 1: _____

_____

Question 2: _____

Answer 2: _____

_____

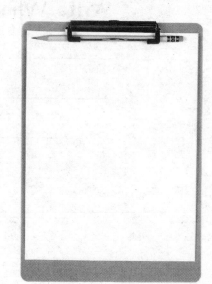

To role-play, pretend to be the person speaking. Practice asking and answering the questions with your partner. Then role-play the interview for the class.

Joe Belanger/123RF.com

Write a Magazine Article

Write a magazine article about the person you interviewed. Be sure to include:

- The person's name

- What he or she does for a living

- Why he or she chose that job

- Why the person thinks the job is important

Quick Tip

Think about interesting details that will help your readers get to know the person better. Be sure to include that information in your article.

COLLABORATE

Talk about your ideas with a partner. Think of an interesting title for the article. Write it here:

_____

Draw an illustration to go with your article. Include a caption.

Nik Merkulov/Shutterstock

My Goal I can read and understand science texts.

TAKE NOTES

Take notes and annotate as you read the passages "Galileo and the Telescope" and "The Shoulders of Giants."

Look for the answer to this question: *How did the two scientists make discoveries?*

_____

_____

_____

_____

_____

PASSAGE 1

EXPOSITORY TEXT

Galileo and the TELESCOPE

Today we take for granted that a telescope helps us see space. But it was not always this way. We can thank Galileo Galilei for giving us a window to the universe.

Galileo was born over 400 years ago in Italy. His father noticed that he was deeply curious about the world. It was no surprise that Galileo grew up to be a scientist.

In 1609, Galileo heard about an invention called a spyglass. This instrument could make faraway things appear near and was invented to spy on wartime enemies. But, Galileo had other ideas for it.

He improved the invention and then pointed his telescope to the sky. Galileo was in awe of what he saw there.

Hulton Archive/Getty Images

At the time, people thought that Earth was at the center of the universe and the Sun and planets orbited it. But, Galileo's observations led him to believe that this was not

Galileo was the first person to see the Moon's craters by using his telescope.

the case. The Sun, he argued, was at the center. Earth and other planets circled the Sun.

The people in power said that Galileo's ideas were dangerous. He was arrested and forbidden from talking about his discoveries. Today, we know Galileo's ideas to be the truth. His work helped us better understand our world.

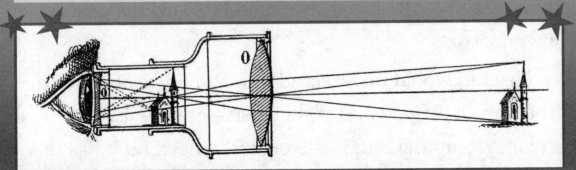

This is a drawing of Galileo's telescope. It could magnify objects 20 times, or make them appear 20 times larger.

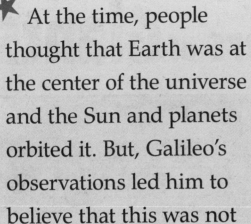

TAKE NOTES

_____

_____

_____

_____

_____

_____

_____

_____

_____

_____

_____

_____

_____

TAKE NOTES

_____

_____

_____

_____

_____

_____

_____

_____

_____

_____

_____

_____

_____

PASSAGE 2 EXPOSITORY TEXT

The Shoulders of Giants

A story is told that Isaac Newton discovered gravity because an apple fell on his head. It is unlikely that this tale is true. But, we do know that the famous scientist asked questions about why an apple falls.

Why does an apple fall down? Why not sideways or up? Newton thought that there must be some force within the Earth that pulls objects toward it. He called this force gravity. All objects are pulled toward the ground by gravity.

Newton would understand how gravity is at work in the universe. Stars and planets have gravity. In our solar system, the Sun is the biggest object. So it has the most gravity. The Sun's gravity keeps the planets in orbit around the Sun.

Isaac Newton knew about gravity on Earth and in space. To learn more, he studied the work of other scientists, including Galileo. Galileo had died near the time that Isaac was born. But Isaac was curious about Galileo's telescope. It had given people their first view of the universe. Newton improved the telescope by adding mirrors. His telescope helped him and other scientists learn even more about the universe.

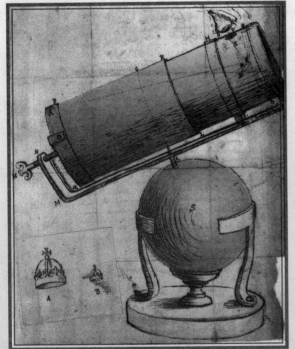

A picture that Newton drew of his telescope

Isaac Newton once said, "If I have seen further it is by standing upon the shoulders of giants." This famous scientist understood that his discoveries were built upon the work of all the great thinkers who came before him.

Science History Images/Alamy Stock Photo

Compare the Passages

Talk About It Reread your notes from "Galileo and the Telescope" and "The Shoulders of Giants." Talk with a partner about how the scientists made their discoveries.

Cite Text Evidence Fill in the Venn diagram with the conclusions each scientist made. Include details that show how the scientists and their discoveries were alike.

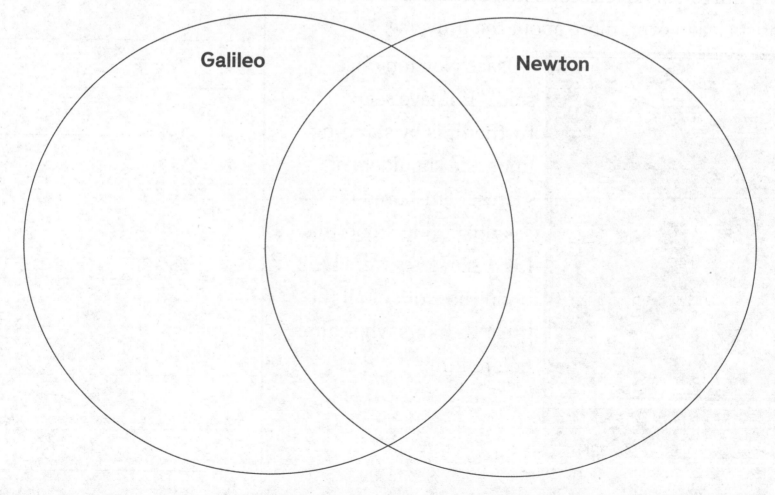

Galileo

Newton

How did the two scientists make discoveries?

 Talk About It Look at the Venn diagram on page 126. Discuss what you learned about Galileo and Newton. Explain how they both came to make discoveries, or conclusions, about the universe.

Write Both scientists _____

_____

_____

_____

_____

> **Quick Tip**
>
> Use these sentence starters to talk about what you learned about the scientists.
>
> *Curiosity led Galileo to...*
>
> *Asking questions helped Newton...*
>
> *Both scientists improved...*
>
> *Both scientists observed...*

 Combine Information

Why is curiosity important for scientists? How can being curious help people learn? What are you curious about? How can you learn more about it?

CHECK IN 1 2 3 4

Gravity Experiment

Gravity is the force that pulls objects down to Earth.

Learn about gravity by doing this experiment.

1. Gather materials. (See sidebar.)

2. Cover the hole with your finger and fill the cup halfway with water.

3. Hold the cup over a sink or bucket. Uncover the hole. What happens? What does this tell you about gravity?

_____

_____

4. Fill the cup again, covering the hole.

5. Drop the cup into the sink or bucket. What do you notice about how the water and the cup fall? What does this tell you about gravity?_____

_____

_____

Talk with your partner about what you learned about gravity. Ask each other questions you still have about gravity and discuss how to find the answers.

Materials

paper cup with hole on the bottom

water

bucket (or sink)

Reflect on Your Learning

Talk About It Reflect on what you learned in this unit. Then talk with a partner about how you did.

I am really proud of how I can _____

_____

_____

_____

Something I need to work more on is _____

_____

_____

_____

_____

Share a goal you have with a partner.

My Goal Congratulations on all that you've accomplished this year! What are your goals for next year? In your reader's notebook, write about what you can do to get there.

Expository Writing Rubric

Score	Purpose, Focus, and Organization (4-point Rubric)	Evidence and Elaboration (4-point Rubric)	Conventions of Standard English (2-point Rubric)
4	• Stays focused on purpose, audience, and task • States the central idea, or main idea • Connects ideas with transitional words • Presents ideas in a logical order • Begins with an introduction and ends with a conclusion that sums up the topic	• Supports the central idea with facts and details • Includes relevant evidence, or supporting details, from the sources • Uses elaborative techniques, such as examples, definitions, and quotations • Expresses ideas clearly with precise language • Uses academic vocabulary to explain the topic • Has different sentence types and lengths	

Score	Purpose, Focus, and Organization (4-point Rubric)	Evidence and Elaboration (4-point Rubric)	Conventions of Standard English (2-point Rubric)
3	• Stays mostly focused on purpose, audience, and task • States a central idea, or main idea that is supported in some parts of the essay • Connects ideas with some transitional words • Presents ideas in a logical order • Begins with an introduction and ends with a conclusion	• Supports the central idea with facts and details • Includes relevant evidence, or supporting details, from some sources • Uses an acceptable amount of different types of details that show understanding of the topic • Expresses ideas with some precise language • Uses some academic vocabulary to explain the topic • Has some different sentence types and lengths	

Expository Writing Rubric

Score	Purpose, Focus, and Organization (4-point Rubric)	Evidence and Elaboration (4-point Rubric)	Conventions of Standard English (2-point Rubric)
2	• Does not stay focused on purpose, audience, and task • States a central, or main, idea that is not supported in the essay • Connects ideas with few transitional words • Does not present ideas in a logical order • Does not have an introduction and/or conclusion	• Supports the central idea with weak facts and details • Includes weak evidence, or supporting details, from few sources • Uses an acceptable amount of different types of details that show understanding of the topic • Expresses ideas with little use of precise language • Uses few academic vocabulary to explain the topic • Has little variety of sentence types and lengths	• Shows understanding of basic grammar and usage conventions • Has some minor errors in word usage, but there is not a pattern of mistakes • Has acceptable usage of punctuation, capitalization, and spelling

Score	Purpose, Focus, and Organization (4-point Rubric)	Evidence and Elaboration (4-point Rubric)	Conventions of Standard English (2-point Rubric)
1	• Does not stay focused on purpose, audience, and task • Does not state a central, or main, idea clearly • Has unrelated ideas and is confusing and unclear • Has few or no transitional words • Is too brief, or short, to show focus or organization	• Shows little support or does not support a central, or main, idea. • Includes little to no use of sources, facts, or details • Expresses ideas that are confusing • Uses few content words or academic vocabulary • Has only short, simple sentences	• Shows some understanding of basic grammar and usage conventions • Has many errors in word usage • Has little or no use of punctuation, capitalization • Has incomplete sentences and many spelling errors
0			• Shows a lack of understanding of grammar and usage conventions • Has many errors that confuse the reader